FLOWERS COLORING BOOK

By: Digital Coloring Books

ISBN: 10: 1983548677
ISBN-13: 978-1983548673

Get More Coloring Books On Demand To Print Off As Many copies as you want at

DigitalColoringBooks.Com

Want to Join our membership site and have access to as many print on demand coloring books. Great for color enthusiasts, teachers, and anyone that likes to save money, for color parties, get togethers, and daily meditative relaxing.

For A Limited Time become a member for $1 trial with promo code, TRYOUT at checkout. Go to

DigitalColoringBooks.Com

More great coloring books here on amazon.com and DigitalColoringBooks.Com

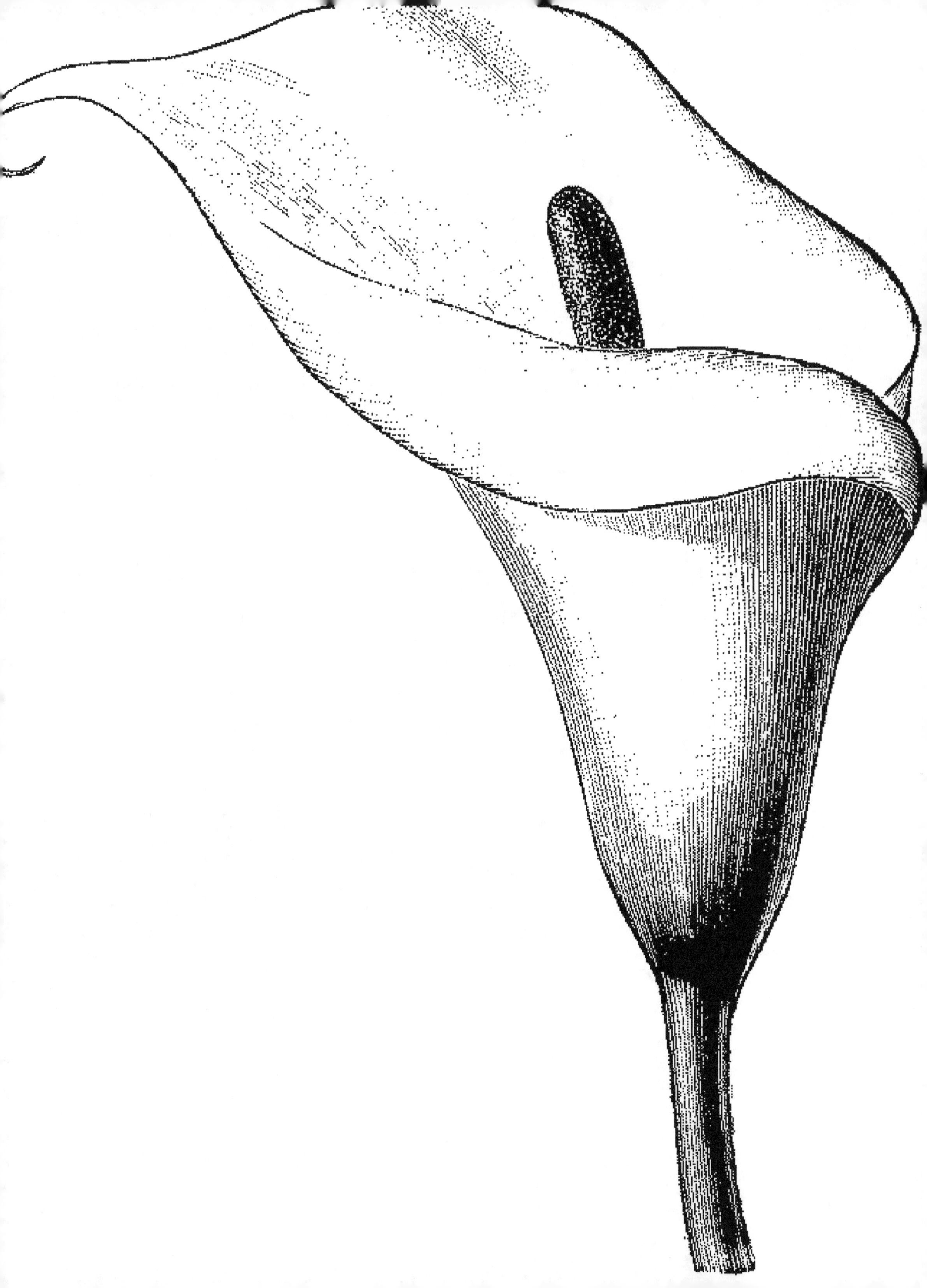

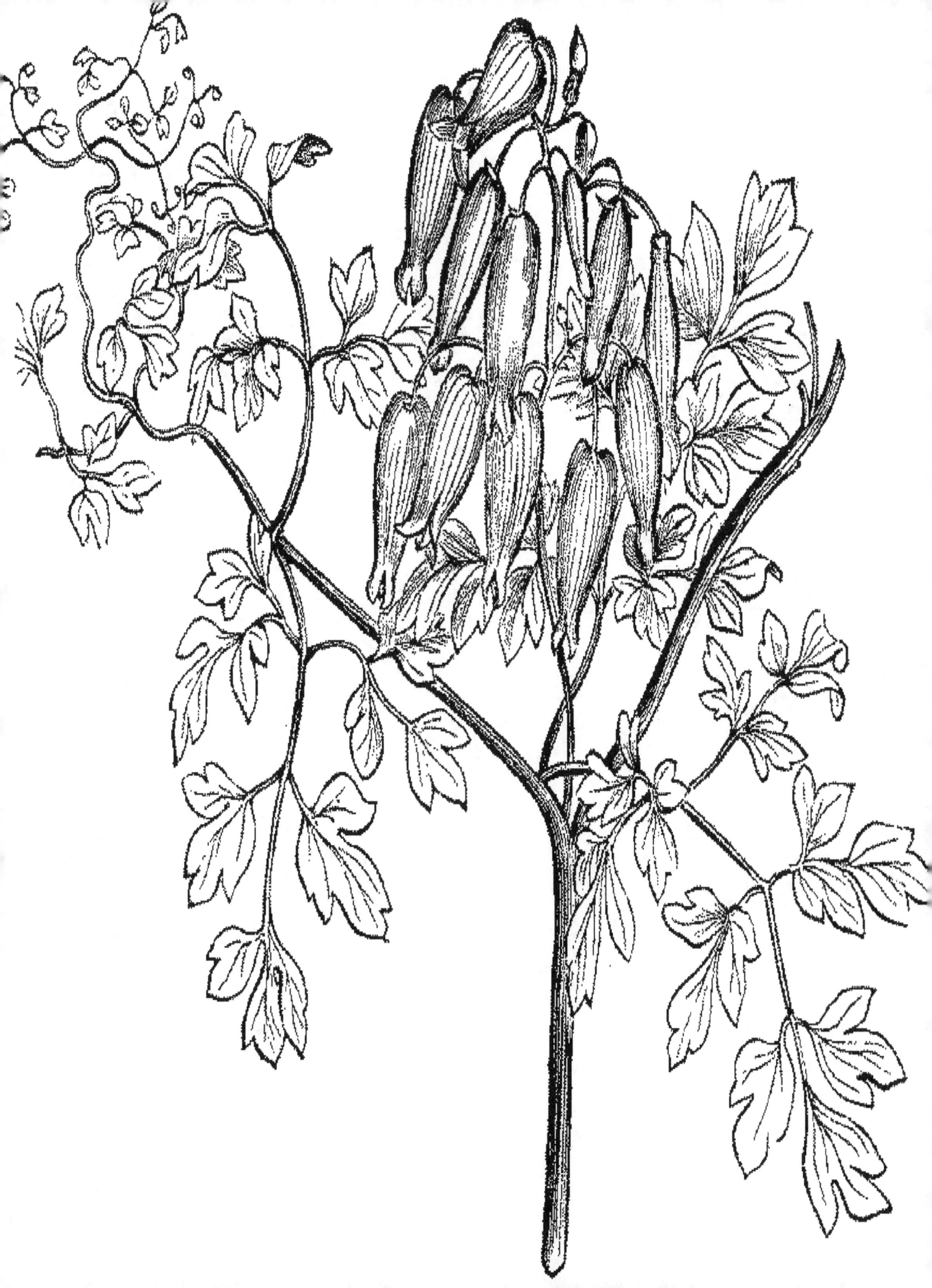

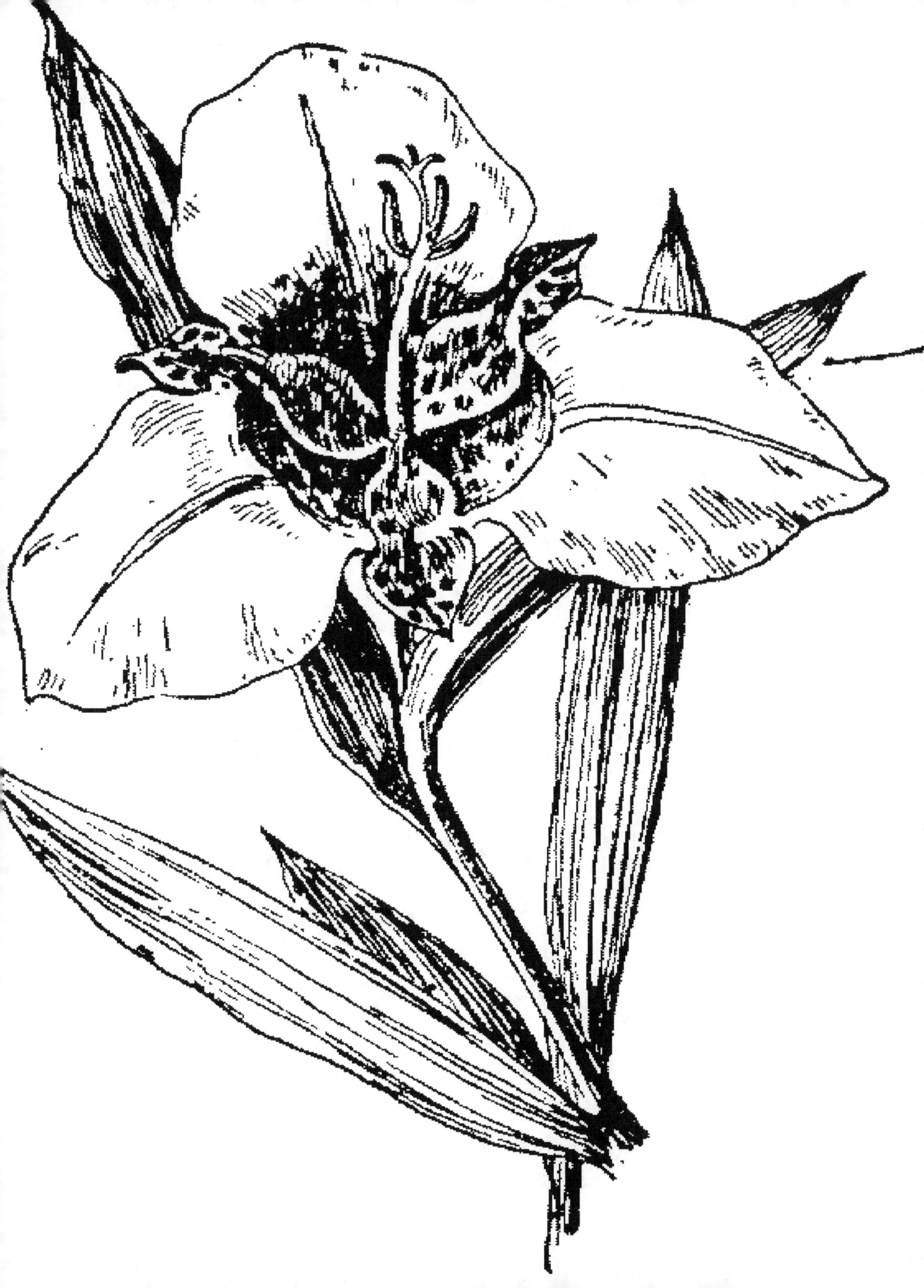

Get More Coloring Books On Demand To Print Off As Many copies as you want at

DigitalColoringBooks.Com

Want to Join our membership site and have access to as many print on demand coloring books. Great for color enthusiasts, teachers, and anyone that likes to save money, for color parties, get togethers, and relaxing.

For A Limited Time become a member for $1 trial with promo code, TRYOUT. Go to

DigitalColoringBooks.Com

More great coloring books here on amazon.com and DigitalColoringBooks.Com